COMIC STRIP SCIENCE

BIOLOGY

Paul Mason and Jess Bradley

Explore the science behind animals, plants and the human body.

WAYLAND

First published in Great Britain in 2022
by Wayland

Copyright © Hodder and Stoughton, 2022

All rights reserved

Editor: Sarah Peutrill
Designer: Lisa Peacock
Science consultant: Penny Coltman

ISBN (HB): 978 1 5263 1998 2
ISBN (PB): 978 1 5263 1999 9

Printed and bound in China

Wayland, an imprint of
Hachette Children's Group
Part of Hodder and Stoughton
Carmelite House
50 Victoria Embankment
London EC4Y 0DZ

An Hachette UK Company
www.hachette.co.uk
www.hachettechildrens.co.uk

Every attempt has been made to clear copyright.
Should there be any inadvertent omission please
apply to the publisher for rectification.

CONTENTS

WHAT IS BIOLOGY?

Biology is the science of living things. Science is about explaining how things work, so biology is about explaining how living things work.

The starting place for any scientific investigation is asking: 'How and why does that happen?' For example:

Why do cows fart so much? (See pages 8–9.)

I do beg your pardon. It was something I ate.

PARP!

Why do people sweat when they're hot? (See page 14.)

How do plants spread their seeds? (See pages 34–35.)

POUF! Ping! Ping! Ping!

Thanks for that!

Look out below!

ANIMALS, PLANTS AND PEOPLE

This book is about animals, plants and people. The comic strips show examples of biology in action – for example:

how a polar bear cares for her cubs ... (See pages 18–19.)

Whoo!

So bright!

Is it my turn yet?

Nope.

Time for you two to leave home.

No, wait ...

• ... how a plant gets shrew poo ... (See pages 38–39.)

I love shrew poo!

and why sneezes aren't simple. (See pages 50–51.)

Achoo!

Around the comic strips you will find science information, plus more examples and explanations of biology in action.

CLASSIFICATION

Living things are grouped using a system we call classification. It is based on what we can see about them, particularly how they are similar and different.

CLASSIFYING FIDO:

KINGDOM
Is it a plant or animal? Have I got leaves?

NO. Animalia.

PHYLUM
Does this animal have a backbone?

Obviously, yes. So I go in Chordata.

CLASS
Does it feed its young milk?

Yes! So I must be a mammal – Mammalia.

WHAT IS AN ANIMAL?

Here are some of the key things that usually make a living thing part of the animal kingdom:

- it cannot make its own food, so it has to eat another living thing to survive

- it breathes in oxygen

- it can move from place to place

COMPARE THESE TO SEE HOW IMPORTANT THE DIFFERENCES AND SIMILARITIES ARE IN CLASSIFICATION.

SPECIES
Does it live with humans?

Totally!
Which make me
Canis familiaris.
A pet dog.

ORDER
Does it eat mostly meat?

Yep.
Which puts me
in Carnivora.

GNAW
GNAW

FAMILY
Did my ancestors have
teeth like these?

Yes = Canidae

GENUS
What is its body shape?

Dog-like = Canis

WHAT IS A PLANT?

These are some of the things that usually make a
living thing part of the plant kingdom:

- it is able to make its own food, using a process
  called photosynthesis (see page 28)

- it takes in carbon dioxide for photosynthesis

- it cannot move from place to place.

EXTREME RECYCLING PLANT EATERS

Plants such as grass do not contain many nutrients. Rabbits are grass-eaters that have found a clever – if revolting – way to make sure they gets all the nutrients they can ...

At sunset, two rabbits have a last snack of the day.

Lovely grass. Munch, munch.

It gets dark. Bedtime for bunnies.

PLIP, PLIP!

PLOP!

PLIP!

During the night, some of the grass reappears at the rabbits' rear ends – as poo.

POO OR SICK?

Rabbits make sure they get ALL the goodness out of their food by pooing it out, then re-eating it. Some other plant eaters regurgitate (or sick up) their food. Then they chew it and swallow it again. These animals include deer, cows, goats and giraffes.

ENERGY FROM PLANTS

Plants contain lots of a thing called cellulose. Inside the plant eater's intestines are bacteria that break up the cellulose to release energy. This causes the plant-eating animal to release a lot of gas (farts)!

8

PLANT-EATER TEETH

Plants are hard to break down. Because of this, most plant eaters have big, flat teeth. These are good for grinding and crushing plants before they are swallowed.

Millions of years ago, plant-eating dinosaurs had teeth like today's plant eaters.

That's disgusting.

Those night-time poos have a few leftover nutrients in them.

Such tasty grass.

Yep.

Second time around, the poos have no nutrients.

Left outside. Even rabbits have standards.

HOW MANY STOMACHS?

Some plant eaters have stomachs divided into four different parts. The food is regurgitated, chewed, and swallowed down to the next stomach. So every meal is sicked up three times. Yuk.

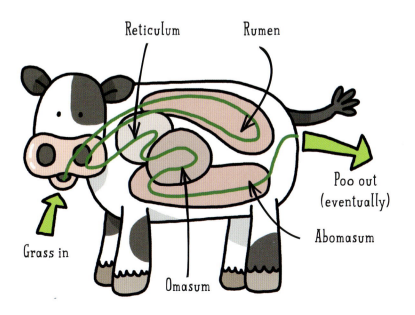

Reticulum

Rumen

Poo out (eventually)

Abomasum

Omasum

Grass in

THE DEADLY EFFECTS OF STAYING UP LATE PREDATORS

Most of us don't like going to bed when we're told to – but if you're a chicken, staying up late can turn out really badly.

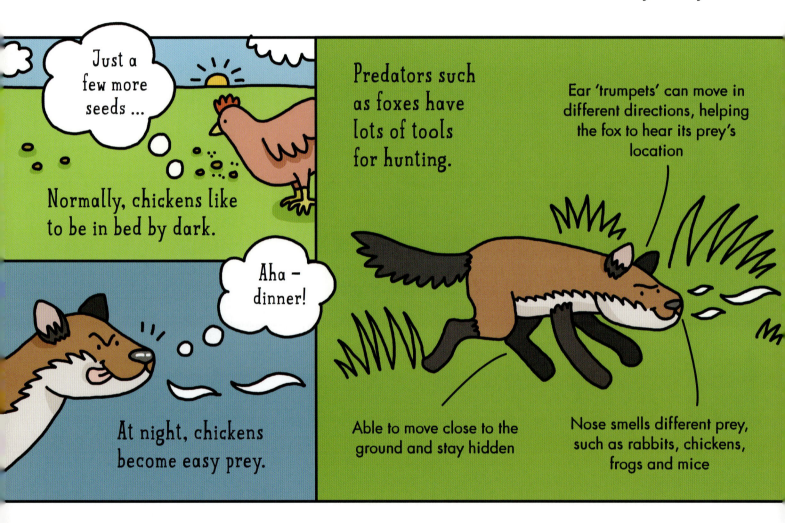

Just a few more seeds ...

Normally, chickens like to be in bed by dark.

Aha – dinner!

At night, chickens become easy prey.

Predators such as foxes have lots of tools for hunting.

Ear 'trumpets' can move in different directions, helping the fox to hear its prey's location

Able to move close to the ground and stay hidden

Nose smells different prey, such as rabbits, chickens, frogs and mice

PREDATOR VISION

Like foxes, many predators have something called 'binocular vision'. This means they have both eyes facing forward. This makes them good at judging distances – they know how far to pounce!

Prey animals often have eyes on the sides of their head to see predators coming from behind as well as in front.

HUNTING WITH SMELL

Many predators use their sense of smell to sniff out a meal. Among the world's best at this are bears:

- polar bears can smell seals through a metre of snow

- grizzly bears follow their nose for over 5 km to find meat.

A bear's nose works about seven times as well as a bloodhound's.

Foxes usually eat some of their prey straight away. Sometimes they store bits of it for later.

TEETH FOR GRIPPING

Foxes have sharp, pointed teeth (called canines) at the front of their mouth. These are perfect for gripping prey to stop it escaping. Many predators have teeth that do a similar job. Sharp, grippy teeth are especially useful for hunting slippery fish — so crocodiles, sharks and dolphins have them too.

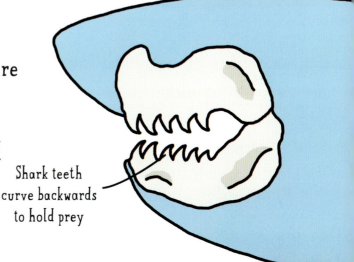

Shark teeth curve backwards to hold prey

11

DON'T COME OUT OF YOUR SHELL!
PROTECTION FROM PREDATORS

Prey animals need to keep themselves safe. But how do you do that if you don't have any claws or fangs and your top speed is about 1.5 kph?

Desert tortoises cannot move very fast.

You go round.

No, YOU go round.

Rival males try to tip each other over with their gular horn.

Gular horn

GNNNN.

RRRRRR.

When a predator appears, tortoises are too slow to run away. Instead they hide inside their hard shell.

Uh oh!

Coyote

Ah, dinner.

PROTECTION 1: SPEED

Some prey animals protect themselves with speed. If they sense a predator, they race away. For example, lions can run for a short time at 80 kph. However, impala, which lions would quite like to eat, can run at 88 kph.

PROTECTION 2: CAMOUFLAGE

Some prey animals try to blend in with their surroundings, so that hungry predators pass right by them. Some do this by matching colours, others with patterns. Masked hunter bugs camouflage themselves by covering their bodies with grains of sand!

PROTECTION 3: ARMOUR

Tortoises are not the only animals that protect themselves with armour. Armadillos, pangolins and some lizards have scaly armour for protection. And Indian rhinoceros have plates of thick, hard skin that work like armour.

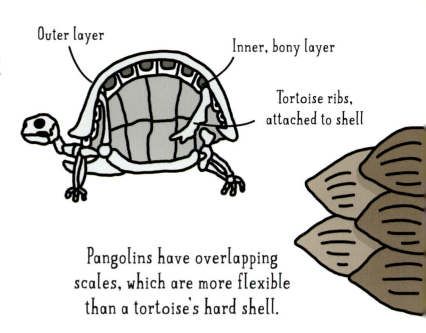

Outer layer

Inner, bony layer

Tortoise ribs, attached to shell

Pangolins have overlapping scales, which are more flexible than a tortoise's hard shell.

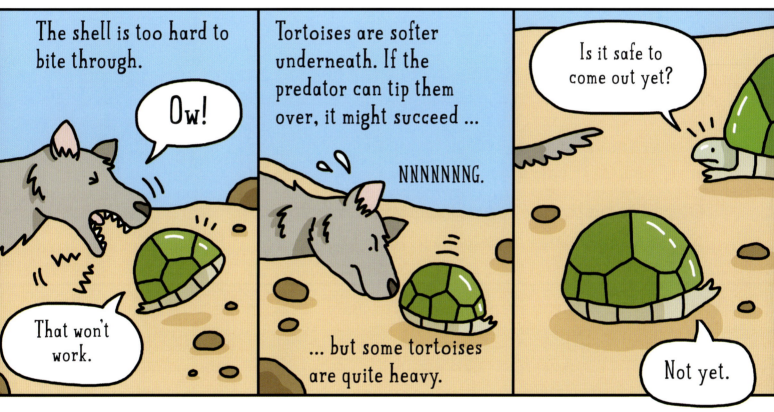

The shell is too hard to bite through.

Ow!

That won't work.

Tortoises are softer underneath. If the predator can tip them over, it might succeed ...

NNNNNNNG.

... but some tortoises are quite heavy.

Is it safe to come out yet?

Not yet.

PROTECTION 4: POISON

A few prey animals protect themselves by being poisonous. Poison dart frogs, for example, have a poisonous coating on their skin. It is so deadly that one tiny frog has enough poison to kill 10 people.

Poisonous animals are often brightly coloured as a warning.

13

CAMELS GET THE HUMP
ANIMALS NEED WATER

All living things need water. Humans are made of about 60% water and need to top it up several times a day*. Some animals, though, can manage without water for a lot longer. *We sweat, breathe, wee and poo out 1-2 litres of water per day.

WATERY JOBS

Inside an animal, water has many jobs.

- Most of the water is inside cells, the tiny building blocks of which living things are made.

- Blood is mainly water, and blood transports energy and nutrients around the body.

- Water helps control the body's temperature, is part of digestion, and helps joints work smoothly.

SIMPLE ANIMAL CELL

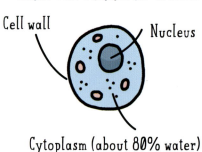

Cell wall

Nucleus

Cytoplasm (about 80% water)

Camels can go weeks without drinking ...

Yes, really.

When camels have plenty to eat and drink, their humps fill with fat.

Plump hump

Slurp! Slurp!

In the desert, finding food and water is difficult.

Phew, it's hot.

Not really.

SALTY CAMELS

Wild camels live in China and Mongolia. They are a different species from other camels. Wild camels are thought to be the ancestors of all other kinds.

There is almost no fresh water where wild camels live, but they have an amazing trick to help them survive. Wild camels can drink salty water – even when it is more salty than seawater.

WATER WITHOUT DRINKING

Some animals that live in very dry places get most of their water without drinking. For example:

- the kangaroo rat lives in the deserts of North America. It can live from just the water inside the seeds the rat eats

- thorny devils survive in the deserts of Australia by sucking water from the ground up grooves in their skin. The grooves then channel the water into the thorny devil's mouth (below).

I was thirsty.

The camel's wide feet stop it sinking into the sand.

An extra, see-through eyelid protects its eye from sand.

Without food or drink, the camel starts to use the fat stored in its humps.

Hump no longer plump

Eventually both humps go floppy. The camel could have lost up to half its weight.

I feel a bit deflated.

Drinking and eating will make the camel healthy again.

SWIMMING IN FISH WEE
SALTY WATER

All living things need water – but if you have ever accidentally taken a slurp of seawater, you'll know that it's too salty to drink*. So what do fish in the sea do?

*Unless you are a wild camel, that is – see page 15 to find out more about that.

As fish swim along, fresh water leaks out of their gills and body.

I'm a bit thirsty.

Gills

Fresh water is pulled out into the salty water outside.

Seawater

More salty

Fish body

Skin

Less salty

To get water, the fish has to drink a LOT of seawater ...

Gulp.
Gulp.
Gulp.

... but then it needs to get rid of the salt.

SALT

Salt does important jobs inside an animal's body. It helps blood, muscles and nerves work properly. Salt also helps living things manage the amount of water in their bodies. We all need salt, but it is important to get the right amount. Not enough is bad for you, and so is too much.

Nice and salty ...

Animals often lick salty rock or clay to get extra salt.

16

FRESHWATER FISH

Freshwater fish have the opposite problem to sea fish. They live in water that is less salty than their bodies – so the salt is always leaking out. They need to take on salt instead of getting rid of it. They do this using their gills. These remove any salt in the water and add it to the fish's blood.

Seawater

Salt out

Fresh water   Gills

Salt in

Sea fish have organs called kidneys, which remove salt.

Kidney

Salt out

The salt is added to the fish's wee and released.

Did you see that?

Disgusting.

This means that every time you go in the sea you are ...

I don't think I want to hear this ...

... swimming in fish wee.

FISHY MIXERS

Some fish are able to survive in seawater and fresh water. Salmon and trout are examples of this. So, worryingly, are bull sharks – one of the few kinds of shark that regularly attacks humans.

One golf course in Australia has bull sharks living in its lake.

DANGER: SHARKS!

Plop!

17

THE MASSIVE MARCH OF A BABY BEAR
MAMMAL LIFE CYCLES

Polar bears are born in a tiny den, then spend the next FOUR MONTHS there. Then they have to do a massive march.

As the weather gets colder, a pregnant female starts to dig a den.

It's a shame last year's den melted.

Inside, she gives birth to two cubs ...

I'm hungry!

So am I!

... which she feeds with milk.*

Inside the den, the bear cubs grow up fast.

They are born with closed eyes and are almost hairless.

Their eyes open after a few weeks.

By eight weeks they can walk around, and have grown thick white fur. Their teeth have appeared.

*Being able to feed young with milk from the mother is one of the things that make mammals mammals.

MAMMALS

Mammals are animals that:
- have backbones
- have fur or hair
- feed their young on mother's milk.

Most mammals also give birth to live young.

AQUATIC MAMMALS

Aquatic mammals live in water. Like all mammals, they feed their young on milk. Aquatic mammals also have lungs, so they need to come to the surface to breathe. All aquatic mammals have hair at some point in their lives too.

MARSUPIALS

Marsupials are mammals that give birth to part-grown young. The young then spend most of their time inside a pouch on their mother, where they feed and grow.

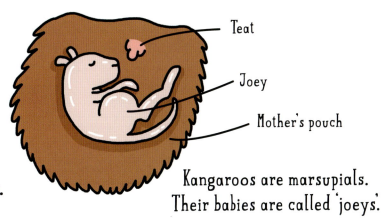

Kangaroos are marsupials. Their babies are called 'joeys'.

Three or four months after they were born, the bears leave their den.

Whoo!

So bright!

Together they walk towards the ice-covered sea. It can be a long journey.

Is it my turn yet?

For two-and-a-half years, their mother teaches the cubs to hunt. Then ...

Time for you two to leave home.

No, wait ...

MONOTREMES

Monotremes are mammals that lay eggs, instead of giving birth to live young. The young still feed on milk like other mammals.

Monotremes include the duck-billed platypus and four different species of echidna. Echidna are small animals a bit like hedgehogs.

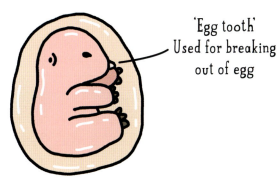

'Egg tooth' Used for breaking out of egg

When they are old enough, monotremes such as this echidna need to break out of their egg.

THE STRANGE JOURNEY OF A BABY TREE FROG
AMPHIBIAN LIFE CYCLES

Amphibians are animals that are born in water, but when they are adults they can live on land and in water.

TYPES OF AMPHIBIAN

There are four main types of amphibian:

- FROGS and TOADS are similar. The easiest way to tell them apart is that frogs have smooth, slippery skin but toads have bumpy, drier skin.

- SALAMANDERS have long, thin bodies. If one of their arms or legs gets bitten or pulled off, they can grow a new one. Newts are a kind of salamander.

- CAECILIANS do not have arms or legs (which saves having to re-grow them when they are pulled off). They look like snakes or worms and can grow as long as 1.5 m.

In spring, a female tree frog climbs down from her tree.

I'll just pop down to the pond.

She lays hundreds of eggs among the pond plants.

About 400, actually.

A male frog comes along to fertilise the eggs ...

Aha! Eggs.

AMPHIBIAN SKIN

Amphibians have amazing skin. It can transport water and gases into and out of the animal. It fights off dangerous bacteria and fungi. Some amphibians also release deadly toxins from their skin. Amphibians need to keep their skin damp, which is why they usually live in wet places.

This yellow-banded poison dart frog has poison glands for protection and mucus glands to keep the skin damp.

Gasp!

A tadpole sticks its mouth out of water to suck air into its lungs before diving back down.

TADPOLE BREATHING

Tadpoles live underwater for eight to ten weeks. They have two ways of breathing. The first way is to grow a set of gills similar to a fish. After a few weeks lungs develop, like the lungs of land animals. Most tadpoles use their lungs and come to the surface to breathe air.

... and little tadpoles start to grow inside them.

I can't wait to get out of here.

After five days, the eggs hatch.

The tadpoles live in water for the next two months.

At the end, they start to grow arms and legs.

METAMORPHOSIS

Once the froglet has front and back legs, it climbs out of the pond ...

This feels like home.

... and up a tree.

FOUR STEPS TO BEING A BUTTERFLY
INSECT LIFE CYCLES

Imagine if your whole body completely changed not once, not twice, or even three, but FOUR times during your life. If that happened, it would mean you were ... an insect. The four stages are egg, larva, pupa and adult, and the transformation is called metamorphosis.

The butterfly starts life as a tiny egg. It is about the same size as this full stop → ·

Inside the egg, a larva* is growing.

When it is big enough, the larva chews a hole in the egg and wriggles out ...

Ngggg! Should have chewed a bigger hole.

... then it eats the rest of the egg ...

... and the leaf the egg was stuck on. The larva eats so much, its skin gets very tight.

MUNCH, MUNCH.

*A larva of a butterfly or moth is sometimes called a caterpillar.

INCOMPLETE METAMORPHOSIS

Some insects have a different life cycle from a butterfly's. Their life cycle has three stages instead of four and is called 'incomplete metamorphosis.'

INCOMPLETE METAMORPHOSIS: LIFE CYCLE OF A DRAGONFLY

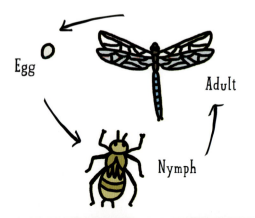

Egg

Adult

Nymph

INVASION OF THE BODY SNATCHERS

Some wasps play a nasty trick on other insects. They find the caterpillar of a butterfly or moth, then inject their eggs into it. The wasp eggs grow, and turn into larvae, feeding on the caterpillar.

Finally, the wasp larvae release chemicals to paralyse the caterpillar. Then each wasp larva cuts itself an escape hatch, using its saw-like teeth.

Wasp larvae cut their way out of a caterpillar.

The skin is shed but another, larger skin is already in place.

That's better.

It will do this four or five more times.

Now the caterpillar attaches itself to a branch, sheds its skin one more time to become ...

I feel like a new me.

... a chrysalis, or pupa.

When the time is right, a butterfly wriggles out of the chrysalis.

I'll just wait for my wings to work.

It pumps up its wings, lets them dry out and flies off.

We're like buses. You wait 17 years, and then millions come along at once.

SEVENTEEN-YEAR CICADAS

Insects take different amounts of time over the stages of their life cycles. Some cicadas spend about eight weeks as an egg, then either 13 or 17 YEARS underground as nymphs. They come to the surface, all at the same time, to become adults, then live for about five more weeks.

THE UNSUITABLE BEDROOM OF A BABY GUILLEMOT
BIRD LIFE CYCLES

Guillemots are seabirds. They spend lots of time out on the ocean. Guillemots return to land to have young, and they build their nests in scary places.

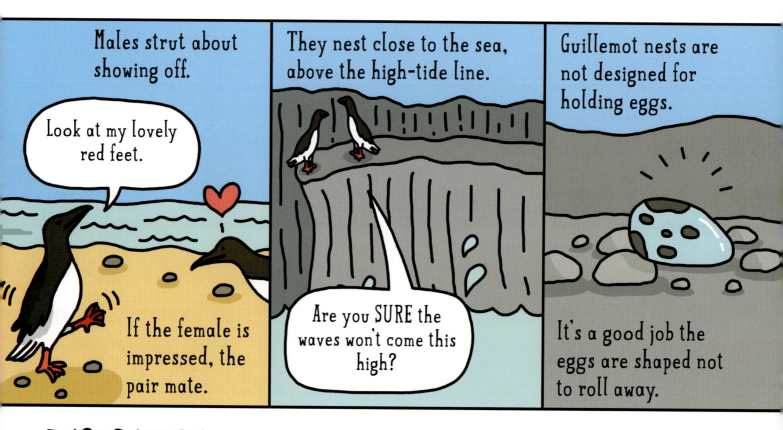

Males strut about showing off.

Look at my lovely red feet.

If the female is impressed, the pair mate.

They nest close to the sea, above the high-tide line.

Are you SURE the waves won't come this high?

Guillemot nests are not designed for holding eggs.

It's a good job the eggs are shaped not to roll away.

INCUBATION

Most birds sit on their eggs to keep them warm. This is called incubation. Without incubation, the chicks growing inside would soon die of cold.

In many birds, a patch of feathers falls out just where the egg touches their skin. The egg gets more warmth because it is touching skin, not feathers.

The egg-warming bare skin is called a 'brood patch'.

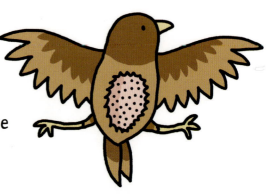

STRANGE SHELLS

Guillemots are not the only birds with unusual eggs.

- Fork-tailed storm petrel eggs are insulated against the cold. This is because the parents have to leave the eggs and fly long distances looking for food.

- Malleefowl bury their eggs to keep them warm. The shells are very thin to let in the ground's warmth.

- Snowy owls live in the Arctic, where the summer sun could be dangerous so their eggshells act like factor 60 sunscreen.

Ostriches lay the bird-world's biggest eggs. They are also very strong to survive having a 100+ kg adult ostrich sitting on them.

The parents take turns sitting on the egg to keep it warm ...

... while inside the egg, the chick grows.

About four weeks after the egg was laid, it hatches.

I was running out of space in there.

About five weeks later, the young guillemot leaves home.

I can't fly yet.

But I can definitely swim.

Aged four, it will be able to have its own chicks.

BIRD SWIMMING CHAMPIONSHIPS

"And the winner is the gentoo penguin, with a top speed of 35 kph."

FLYING UNDERWATER

Guillemots can fly, but they are better swimmers. They use their wings to 'fly' through water. Guillemots often go 30–60 m underwater to find food, and sometimes further. Penguins, cormorants, shags and lots of other birds also 'fly' underwater.

DINNERTIME IN THE OCEAN
FOOD CHAINS

Food chains show how living creatures depend on each other for food. Plants are at the start of food chains. At the other end is an apex predator.

LEVEL 1: PHYTOPLANKTON

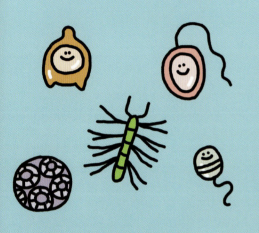

Phytoplankton are tiny ocean plants. There are about 5,000 different kinds.

LEVEL 2: HERBIVORES

Tiny animals called zooplankton eat the phytoplankton ...

... and bigger animals eat other ocean plants.

Munch, munch.

SMALL PLANTS WITH A BIG JOB

Phytoplankton may be tiny but they do two very important jobs. Like green plants on land, they produce oxygen (see page 28). Phytoplankton are also at the start of almost every food chain in the ocean.

Plankton

Shrimps

Small fish

Bigger fish

Seal

Great white shark

We use arrows to show what eats what in a food chain.

26

PLANTS ARE PRODUCERS

In a food chain, plants are called 'producers'. They are called this because, unlike animals, plants produce their own food.

ANIMALS ARE CONSUMERS

Animals in a food chain are called 'consumers'. They cannot make their own food, as plants can. So animals have to consume (which is another word for 'eat') food from outside their bodies.

LEVEL 3: CARNIVORES
Small fish eat the zooplankton.

Where's Bob?

I'm here.

They often band together in shoals for safety.

LEVEL 4: APEX PREDATORS
Small fish get eaten by bigger fish, until ...

Ahhhh!

Lunchtime!

Glad I missed breakfast.

... at the end of the food chain is something too big to be eaten.

PREDATOR AND PREY

Prey animals are eaten by others. An animal that eats prey animals is a predator. Sometimes, though, a predator meets a bigger predator and gets eaten. It has become prey ...

Apex (or top) predators don't have to worry about being eaten. They include great white sharks, lions and polar bears. The only animal that regularly kills top predators is humans.

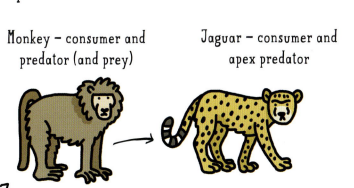

Grass – producer

Grasshopper – consumer and prey

Monkey – consumer and predator (and prey)

Jaguar – consumer and apex predator

27

BURIED ALIVE!
HOW PLANTS GROW

Imagine starting life buried underground. Your first job would be tunnelling your way out. For many plants, that is just how life begins.

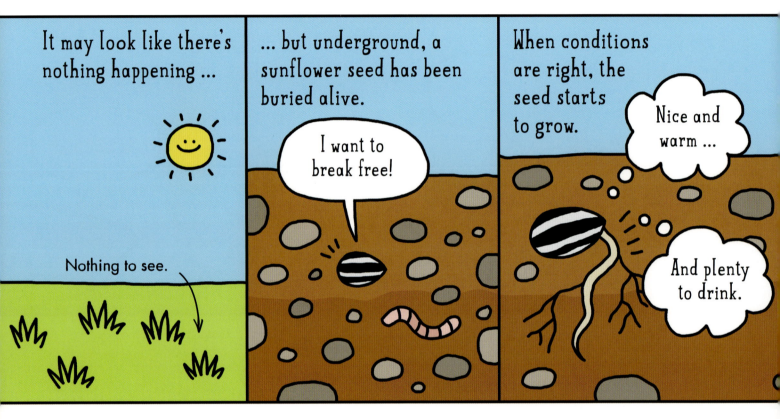

It may look like there's nothing happening ...

Nothing to see.

... but underground, a sunflower seed has been buried alive.

I want to break free!

When conditions are right, the seed starts to grow.

Nice and warm ...

And plenty to drink.

LEAVES

A plant's leaves have a very important job. Plants do not have to find food, like us. Instead, their leaves make food for the plant. They do this using sunlight, water and a gas called carbon dioxide. This is called photosynthesis.

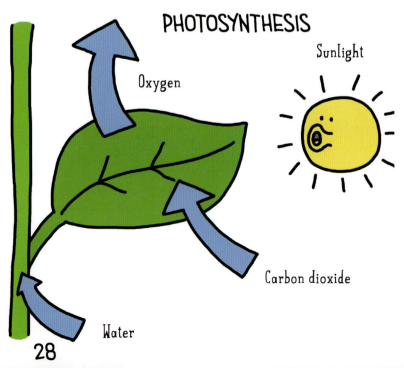

PHOTOSYNTHESIS

Oxygen

Sunlight

Carbon dioxide

Water

WATER

Plants need water to stay alive and grow. They mainly get water through their roots (see page 36). These dig down into the ground until they find wet soil. Then they suck in the water. It goes up the plant's stem to its leaves.

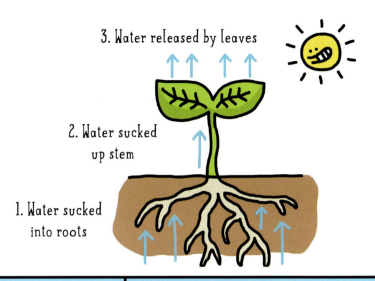

3. Water released by leaves

2. Water sucked up stem

1. Water sucked into roots

The plant grows up and up. Its leaves open to the sun.

Phew! Nice to sunbathe a bit.

Stem

Roots

The flower opens.

Those look tasty ...

Sunflower seeds

The seeds get eaten and ... released.

Bombs away!

The seeds sink into the soil, ready for next year.

NUTRIENTS

Plants use their roots to collect nutrients, as well as water. They collect three main nutrients:

- nitrogen – for healthy leaves, stems and branches

- phosphorus – for seed germination and root development

- potassium – helps flower and fruit production and helps the plant to resist disease.

29

THE (PLANT) WORLD'S BIGGEST STINKER
WHAT FLOWERS ARE FOR

Meet the titan arum, a plant that takes years to make a flower. When it finally does, anyone nearby wishes they were somewhere else ...

It's years since I flowered ...

The plant lurks underground.

Every few years, it pushes up a spike.

That wasn't there last week.

A week later, the flower opens ...

WHIFF
STINK
PONG

... it smells like rotting flesh.

What is that LOVELY smell?

Oh, that is BAD. Let's go.

FLOWERS
Even though flowers from different plants do not look the same, most have the same parts.

PARTS OF A FLOWER

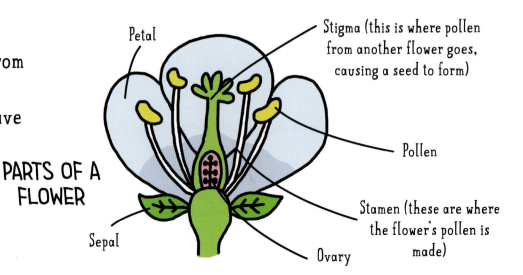

Petal

Stigma (this is where pollen from another flower goes, causing a seed to form)

Pollen

Stamen (these are where the flower's pollen is made)

Sepal

Ovary

30

POLLINATION

Flowering plants reproduce by pollination. This happens when pollen is carried from one flower to another. The pollen of most flowers is carried by insects, or sometimes birds. They are attracted to the flowers by colour or scent. This tells them that at the base of the flower's petals there is a drink of sweet nectar to be found. The pollen of some plants, including many crops, grass and some kinds of trees, is carried by the wind.

The local flies try to visit as many titan arums as they can ...

... pollinating them on their travels.

A day later, the flower starts to disappear and little fruits appear.

These are delicious!

Num, num, num ...

NON-FLOWERING PLANTS

Not all plants use flowers to reproduce. Some trees grow cones made of tightly packed seeds. When the seeds are released, the wind blows them away.

Mosses and ferns spread using 'spores'. These are tiny living things, usually with only one cell. The wind can blow them long distances without animal helpers.

TREE CONES

A POLLEN FACIAL FOR BIRDS
POLLEN DISTRIBUTION

Some plants have amazingly clever ways of spreading their pollen around. Axinaea affinis, for example, offers birds a snack ... and a pollen facial.

Axinaea affinis has a strange-shaped stamen (see page 30).

Hollow bulb

Tube

Opening

A hungry bird makes a grab for the stamen.

Hmm, all sugary and sweet.

POLLINATION TRAPS

Some plants trap insects to help the plant pollinate. Bucket orchids, for example, produce oil that a particular bee REALLY likes. Male bees rub themselves in the oil, hoping it will attract females.

Do you like my scent?

If bees fall into the orchid's water-filled bowl, the only way out is up an escape hatch (which has bee-sized steps). As the bees squeeze through, they collect pollen or leave it behind.

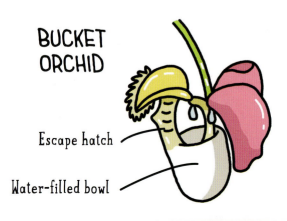

BUCKET ORCHID

Escape hatch

Water-filled bowl

POLLINATION TRICKS

Some plants trick insects into helping them with pollination. The ones that smell like rotting meat (see page 30–31) are doing this. Other plants disguise themselves – for example, by having flowers that look like a female bee. When male bees come to investigate, they get covered in pollen.

As its beak closes, the bulb collapses like an air-filled paper bag ...

The bird carries on feeding ...

Num, num, num ...

... and a cloud of pollen sprays out of the tube, all over the bird's face.

I was NOT expecting that.

... and the pollen drops off its face and into the flower.

POLLINATION AT SEA

Seagrasses are flowering plants that live underwater. Birds and insects cannot help with pollination.

Instead, the plants release pollen that can float beneath the surface. It stays there for days, waiting to find a seagrass plant to land on.

SEAGRASS

THE ADVENTUROUS JOURNEY OF A COCONUT
SPREADING SEEDS

Plant seeds move away from home to find a place of their own to live. They have lots of ways to do this – but not many are as adventurous as a coconut.

Somewhere on a tropical island ...

... a coconut seed falls from the tree ...

THWOCK!
BOUNCE
BOUNCE
BOUNCE

... rolls into the sea ...

... and floats off.

BLOWING IN THE WIND

Lots of plant seeds are spread by the wind. Some trees, such as maples, even have wing-shaped seeds. These help the seeds spin off into the distance as they fall from the tree.

CANNONBALL SEEDS

A few plants have found an excellent way to spread their seeds. They fire them out like a cannonball. This is called 'ballistic' seed spreading. Chinese witch hazel is one of the best ballistic spreaders around.

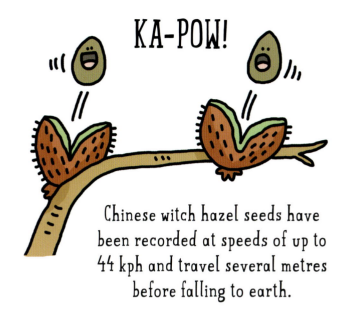

KA-POW!

Chinese witch hazel seeds have been recorded at speeds of up to 44 kph and travel several metres before falling to earth.

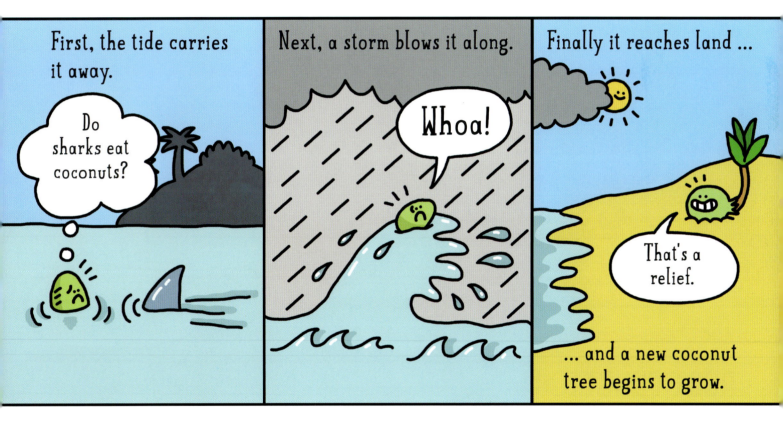

First, the tide carries it away.

Do sharks eat coconuts?

Next, a storm blows it along.

Whoa!

Finally it reaches land ...

That's a relief.

... and a new coconut tree begins to grow.

ANIMAL HELPERS

Animals often help plants spread their seeds – usually in poo. The animal eats the seed, or a fruit with seeds inside it. The seed passes through the animal's digestive system and is pooed out later, somewhere else.

GERMINATION

Germination is the name for the time when a seed starts to grow. It happens when there is just the right amount of sunlight, warmth, air and water.

THE TOUGH LIFE OF A SHEPHERD TREE ROOTS

Plants cannot grow without water and nutrients. But what happens if you live in a desert? You have to dig down deep – just ask the shepherd tree.

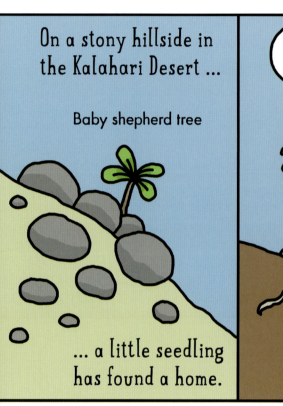

On a stony hillside in the Kalahari Desert ...

Baby shepherd tree

... a little seedling has found a home.

I could do with a drink.

The tree sends its roots deep underground.

The roots may grow down 70 m.

That's as tall as 14 giraffes!

ROOT FUNCTION

Roots do two main jobs for a plant. The most important is to draw in water and nutrients from the soil (see page 29). Without these the plant cannot survive.

Roots also hold the plant in place. If an animal crashes past, or the wind blows hard, the roots (and stem) stop the plant falling over.

ROOTS ARE WATER DETECTORS

Some plant roots have a very useful skill – they can pick up vibrations of running water. The scientists who discovered this found out that the plants were actually even cleverer. The plants can tell the difference between natural water (which they like) and tap water (which they do not).

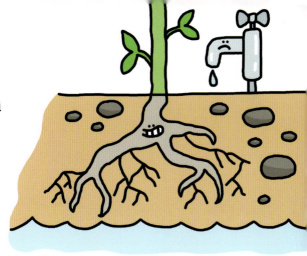

The shepherd tree has put in a lot of effort – and the local animals get the rewards.

Ow!

MUNCH! MUNCH!

Giraffes eat the top leaves.

Termites build their mounds near, and sometimes leaning on, the trunks.

Trees are excellent scaffolding.

The berries can be eaten. The roots can even be used to make a hot drink - a *bit* like coffee.

SLURP!

Hi! ☻

(NOT) INSTANT MESSAGING

Some plants – especially trees – can talk to each other using their root systems. They send messages using chemicals, and even sometimes very slow pulses of electricity.

Beech trees use the root network to share nutrients and water. Sometimes, neighbours that have been cut down are kept alive for years by other trees.

THE TREE SHREW AND ITS HELPFUL POO
PLANT NUTRITION

Plants need sunlight, air, water and nutrients. Many plants get their nutrients from soil – but this pitcher plant has a different method.

Nepenthes rajah lives in the mountains of Borneo.

Bowl holds up to two litres of water.

A tree shrew arrives ...

'Lid' and rim of bowl covered in sweet nectar

Sniff! Sniff!

... and jumps up for a sweet snack.

Lick!

Slurp!

FARMING WITH POO

Poo contains nutrients that help plants grow, including:

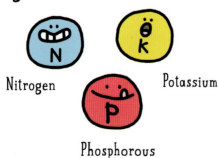

Nitrogen

Potassium

Phosphorous

Farmers have been adding poo to their crops for thousands of years. Anglo-Saxons used to put animal poo on their fields in February. In Japan, human poo was used. Wealthy people had better food, so there were more nutrients in their poo and it was more valuable.

CARNIVOROUS PLANTS

Some plants live where the soil does not contain many nutrients. A few of them are carnivorous – meat-eaters. Usually they eat insects, trapping them and then taking in nutrients from the insect's body. *Nepenthes rajah* is carnivorous, because it eats insects as well as shrew poo.

When the fly lands on the Venus flytrap's 'trap', the trigger hairs will make it snap shut.

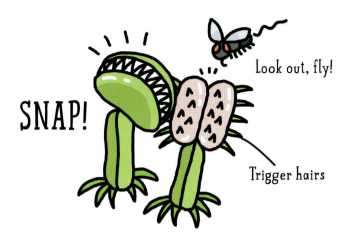

SNAP!

Look out, fly!

Trigger hairs

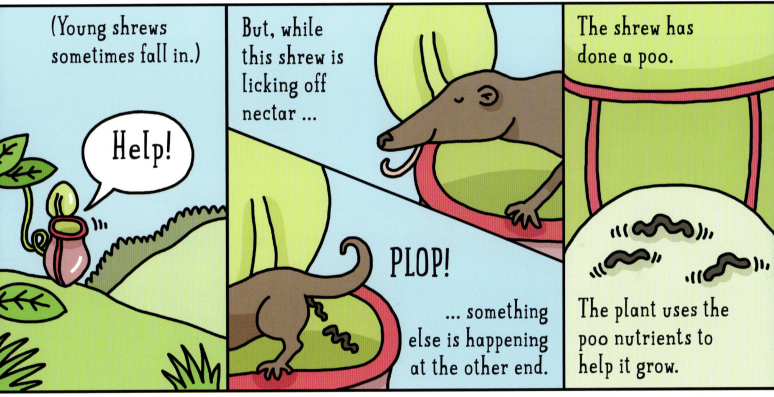

(Young shrews sometimes fall in.)

Help!

But, while this shrew is licking off nectar ...

PLOP!

... something else is happening at the other end.

The shrew has done a poo.

The plant uses the poo nutrients to help it grow.

MUTUALISM

Mutualism is the word for when two different species gain something by working together. In the comic strip, *Nepenthes rajah* gains nutrients and the tree shrew gains a meal.

The world is full of mutualism. For example, there are tiny bacteria living inside you that help you digest your food and get a meal in return.

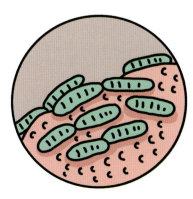

Bacteria help humans digest food in their intestines.

PLANTS AND THE PLANET
THE GREENHOUSE EFFECT

Plants do a crucial job for our planet. They help control how hot or cold it is because of something called the greenhouse effect.

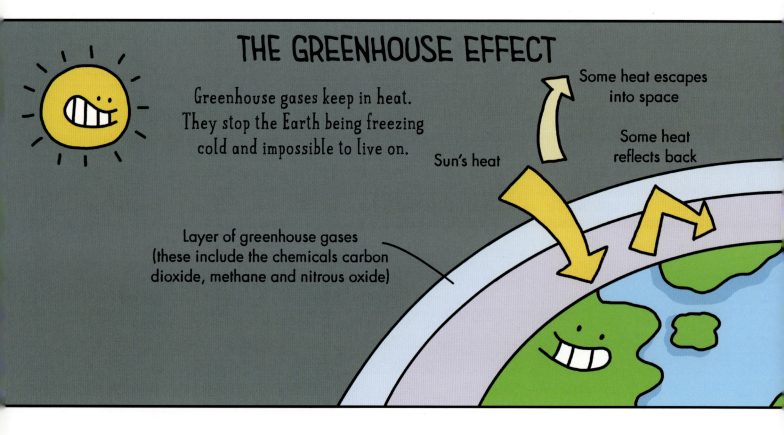

THE GREENHOUSE EFFECT

Greenhouse gases keep in heat. They stop the Earth being freezing cold and impossible to live on.

Sun's heat

Some heat escapes into space

Some heat reflects back

Layer of greenhouse gases (these include the chemicals carbon dioxide, methane and nitrous oxide)

CARBON IN PLANTS

Plants take in carbon dioxide as part of making their own food (see page 28). Carbon is not only stored in living plants. There is also carbon in dead phytoplankton at the bottom of the sea, and in the fossil fuels coal, oil, gas and peat. Forests, in particular, often take in more carbon than they release.

FUELLING THE GREENHOUSE

Today, we get a lot of our energy by burning plants or ex-plants. Many people burn wood for heat and cooking. Power stations burn coal, oil or gas for electricity.

When they are burned, plants release their carbon into the air. Some ends up in the greenhouse layer. Once there, it adds to global warming.

Carbon dioxide

Carbon dioxide

THE GREENHOUSE EFFECT TODAY

Less heat escapes into space

More heat is reflected back

Today, the amount of greenhouse gases in the atmosphere has increased.

Overall, the Earth's temperature is rising. It has already risen by 1°C, and experts think it will rise more. This is called global warming.

GREENHOUSE+

In the 1800s, humans began to burn larger and larger amounts of fossil fuel. The carbon dioxide and other gases that have been released have created a kind of greenhouse+ effect. The effect of this is global warming.

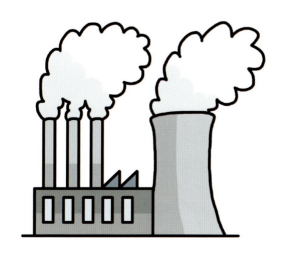

A CHANGING WORLD
CHANGING HABITATS AND THEIR EFFECT

The world's climate is getting warmer. This is having a big effect on the habitats of animals and plants.

THE ARCTIC

In the Arctic, the sea ice is there for less of the year. Seals need the ice to raise their young. Seals are polar bears' main food and without seals, the bears starve. With less ice and seals, polar bears now have to walk or swim long distances to find somewhere to hunt.

I'm sure it wasn't this far last year ...

Deserts have become hotter and drier. Desert animals and plants can survive very high temperatures and weeks without water, but even these plants and animals are struggling now.

DESERTS

The world's deserts are spreading. Deserts are places with very little water, where few plants or animals can survive. As deserts spread, the living things that once lived on the edge lose their homes.

I hear it's cooler on higher ground.

OCEANS

Rising temperatures have caused sea levels to rise. Melted ice has flowed into the oceans. Water also takes up more room when it is warmer. In some places, coastal land is now regularly flooded by seawater. The salt in the water kills the plants, makes the soil infertile and drives out animals.

Coral reefs are also suffering. When sea temperatures rise, the colourful corals turn white and start to die. They can recover, but only if the temperature returns to normal.

This used to be such a colourful reef.

SUPER STORMS

In different places, super storms are called hurricanes, cyclones or typhoons. They are storms with wind strong enough to rip the roofs off buildings. The waves that come with a super storm can eat away the coast and rain can cause floods. All of this affects plants, animals and humans.

Birds can be blown off course by hurricanes, carrying them as much as 2,000 km from home.

Whoa!

Where am I?

USA: 2,000 KM

Super storms begin over the sea. The sea temperature has to be at least 27.8°C for a storm to begin. As more parts of the sea reach this temperature, there will be more storms in the future.

THE FAT CONTROLLER
THE BRAIN

This Fat Controller is not Sir Topham Hatt (who is in charge of Thomas the Tank Engine's railway). It is your brain – which is nearly 60% fat.

BRAIN JOBS

Human brains do a lot, for example:

- automatically controlling things without being instructed to, such as your heartbeat

- processing signals from your senses, such as working out what you are looking at

- managing things like running, singing or kicking a ball

- processing thoughts, emotions and how you behave towards other people.

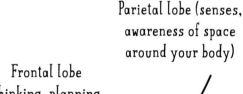

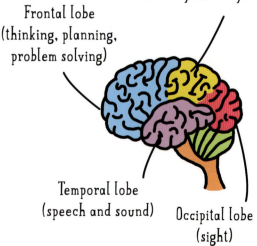

Parietal lobe (senses, awareness of space around your body)

Frontal lobe (thinking, planning, problem solving)

Temporal lobe (speech and sound)

Occipital lobe (sight)

44

THE NERVOUS SYSTEM

Your brain gets and sends its messages using the nervous system. This is a network that sends signals around your body. The signals pass up and down your spinal cord, which is inside your backbone.

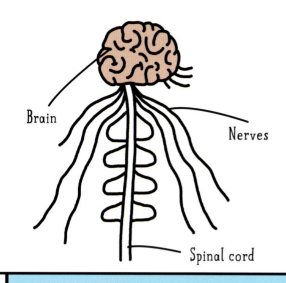

Brain

Nerves

Spinal cord

The brain gets the hot-sand message and sends two messages back.

Message 1: stop touching the hot sand.

Waaaa!

Message 2: get to the cool sea, otherwise you'll have burned feet.

That's better. I wonder how I'll get back ...

The brain has come to the rescue.

A NEURON

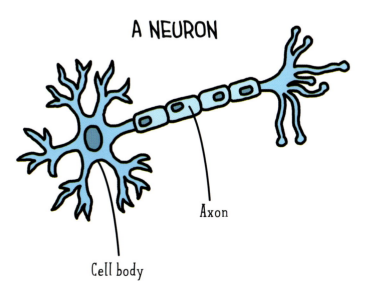

Axon

Cell body

NEURONS

The brain and nervous system work using special cells called neurons. Neurons have two key parts:

- the cell body, which uses electricity to send signals

- the axon, which connects to other neurons, carrying signals.

THE DIFFERENCE BETWEEN A HUMAN AND A JELLYFISH
BONES AND THE SKELETON

Actually, there are a LOT of differences between a human and a jellyfish. One of the most important, though, is that humans have a skeleton giving them shape.

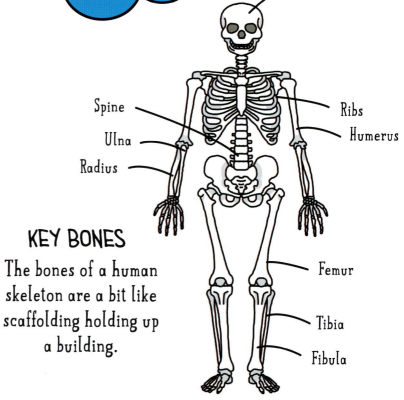

Skull
Spine
Ulna
Radius
Ribs
Humerus
Femur
Tibia
Fibula

KEY BONES
The bones of a human skeleton are a bit like scaffolding holding up a building.

Our skeletons make all kinds of things possible ...

It's very important that I pick this up.

... including some slightly strange ones.

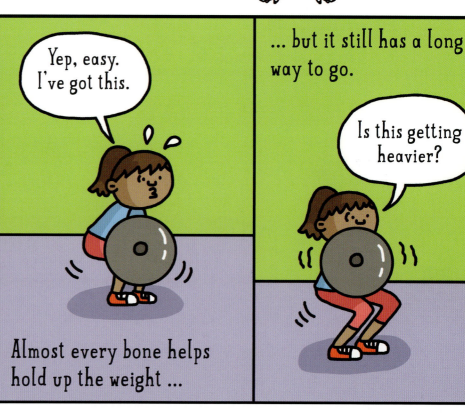

Yep, easy. I've got this.

Almost every bone helps hold up the weight ...

... but it still has a long way to go.

Is this getting heavier?

PROTECTION

Bones are not only used to hold up our bodies. They also provide protection for some of the important organs inside us. The most important is the skull, acting as a built-in helmet for our brains. Our ribs form a cage that stops our lungs and heart being crushed.

A grown-up's skull can withstand nearly 500 kg of pressure ...

It is NOT a good idea to test this.

BROKEN BONES

When bones break, they do not stay broken. First, lots of blood rushes to the break and delivers the cells that are needed to heal it. Over the next few weeks, new bone begins to grow, linking the broken bits together. Eventually this hardens and the bone is repaired.

47

HOW TO BECOME A WORLD ARM-WRESTLING CHAMPION
MUSCLES

To beat other people at arm wrestling, you need strong arms – and for strong arms, you need strong arm muscles ...

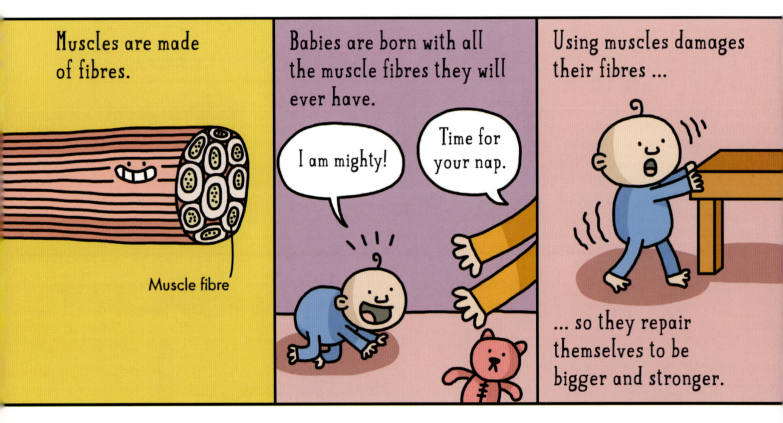

Muscles are made of fibres.

Muscle fibre

Babies are born with all the muscle fibres they will ever have.

I am mighty!

Time for your nap.

Using muscles damages their fibres ...

... so they repair themselves to be bigger and stronger.

MUSCLE MOVEMENT

The muscles in our bodies help us move. They are attached to our bones either side of the joints where two bones meet. When a muscle tightens or contracts, it pulls on the bone to make it move.

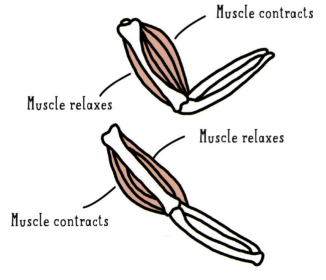

Muscle contracts

Muscle relaxes

Muscle relaxes

Muscle contracts

SKELETAL MUSCLES

The muscles that move our joints are called skeletal muscles. Muscles and bones are connected by tough, strong attachments called tendons. (Bones are connected to other bones by ligaments.)

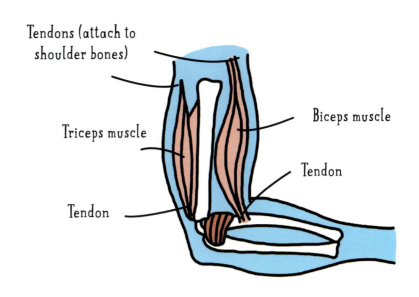

Tendons (attach to shoulder bones)

Biceps muscle

Triceps muscle

Tendon

Tendon

Every time muscles work hard, their fibres become stronger ...

Gnnnnn!

... but without use, they grow weaker.

WAP!

PING!

DAK-A-DAK-A-DAK-A!

If your muscles keep getting bigger and stronger, you might one day make it to the world championships ...

... even if it's only as a spectator!

SMOOTH MUSCLES

Smooth muscle is found in the walls of hollow parts of the human body. The throat and intestines, for example, have walls of smooth muscle. It contracts and relaxes to force food through the digestive system. This is called peristalsis.

PERISTALSIS

The muscles contract and relax to squeeze food along, a bit like squeezing a tube of toothpaste.

THE COMPLICATED STORY OF A SIMPLE SNEEZE
DISEASES AND THE LUNGS

Sneezes are a way for your body to keep out irritating things it does not like.* A sneeze seems like a simple thing – but it is not.

*You can sneeze out pollen, dust, bacteria and viruses, but not irritating younger brothers/sisters or homework.

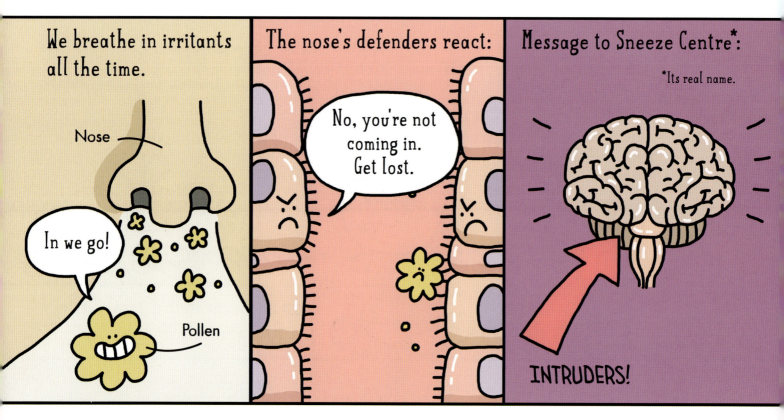

We breathe in irritants all the time.

Nose

In we go!

Pollen

The nose's defenders react:

No, you're not coming in. Get lost.

Message to Sneeze Centre*:

*Its real name.

INTRUDERS!

SNEEZES AND DISEASES

Sneezes are one of the ways the body keeps out sickness. Viruses and bacteria get caught up in the mucus lining the nose, then sneezed out.

A-CHOO!

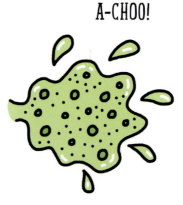

However, sneezes are also one of the ways diseases spread. When the mucus sprays out, it can be picked up by other people. This is why you should always sneeze (and cough) into a tissue or your elbow.

LUNGS

We have one lung on each side of the body and this is where the air for a sneeze comes from. But their main jobs are bringing oxygen into the body and releasing carbon dioxide.

Lungs are made up of about 2,000 km of airways. Both lungs are protected by the rib cage but this diagram shows the right lung without this.

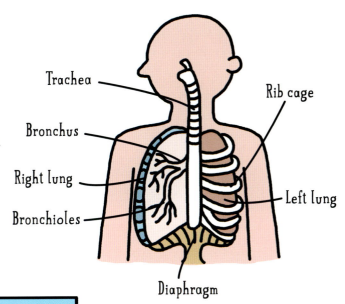

Trachea

Bronchus

Right lung

Bronchioles

Rib cage

Left lung

Diaphragm

Message from Sneeze Centre: **SNEEZE!**

To make a sneeze happen, the Sneeze Centre has to make a lot of things happen very quickly:

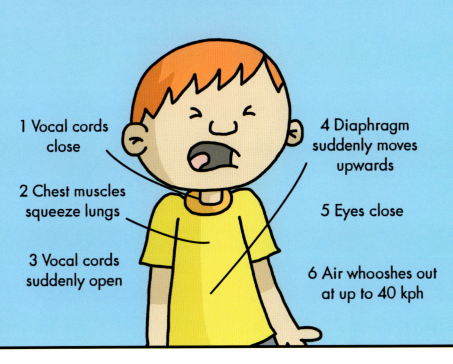

1 Vocal cords close

2 Chest muscles squeeze lungs

3 Vocal cords suddenly open

4 Diaphragm suddenly moves upwards

5 Eyes close

6 Air whooshes out at up to 40 kph

AAAA-CHOO!

WHOOSH!

WHOA!

DIAPHRAGM

The diaphragm is a sheet of muscle at the bottom of the lungs. It makes breathing possible.

BREATHING IN

Air sucked into lungs

Rib cage moves out

Diaphragm contracts and moves down

BREATHING OUT

Air pushed out of lungs

Rib cage moves in

Diaphragm relaxes and curves back up

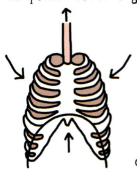

A CLOSE ENCOUNTER OF THE COBRA KIND
HEART AND CIRCULATORY SYSTEM

Imagine: you are walking through the Indian countryside one day and you hear a slithery rustling noise. And then you hear a hiss ...

It's not a grass snake ...

I was asleep!

... it's a cobra.

First, you freeze.

Oh, no.

Your brain gets to work, sending messages:

Heart: beat faster.

Lungs: breathe more

Muscles: prepare for extreme effort

REACTION TO DANGER

When humans meet something dangerous, it sets off an automatic response. The circulatory system goes into overdrive. We breathe faster to get more oxygen, which will power our muscles. The heart beats quicker, rushing oxygen (and energy-rich sugars) to the muscles. Blood even gets thicker, so that if we are injured it will clot more quickly.

THE CIRCULATORY SYSTEM

The circulatory system is a network of blood vessels. Blood is pumped around the body transporting three important things:

1) oxygen from the lungs

2) carbon dioxide to the lungs

3) nutrients from the digestive system.

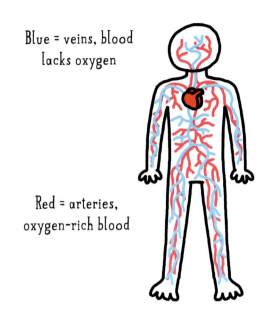

Blue = veins, blood lacks oxygen

Red = arteries, oxygen-rich blood

Step back slowly ...

HISSsss

AHHHHHH!

... and now run away!

Once you are somewhere safe, tell your friends what happened.

No, I was never scared.

HUMAN HEART

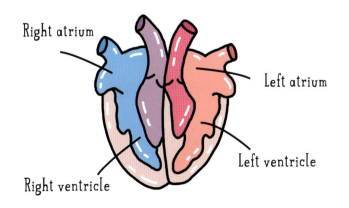

Right atrium

Left atrium

Left ventricle

Right ventricle

THE HEART

The heart is made of muscle and it squeezes and relaxes to pump blood around the circulatory system.

The right side of your heart receives the blood that has just travelled round your body and has had the oxygen removed. It pumps the blood to your lungs (see page 51) to collect oxygen. The left side of your heart pumps the oxygen-rich blood round your body again.

THE LIFE AND TIMES OF A RED BLOOD CELL
FUNCTIONS OF THE BLOOD

Imagine having a job that you had to do non-stop (without sleep!) for four months. That is what life is like for a red blood cell.*

*Fortunately they do have trillions of fellow workers to help.

CAPILLARIES

Capillaries are tiny blood vessels where blood collects and delivers its loads. Chemicals pass into and out of the blood through tiny openings in the capillary walls. The biggest capillaries are only 10% as wide as a human hair. The smallest one is half that size.

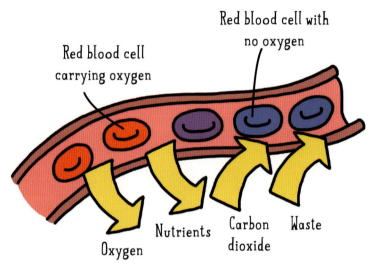

Red blood cell carrying oxygen

Red blood cell with no oxygen

Oxygen   Nutrients   Carbon dioxide   Waste

INSIDE A CAPILLARY

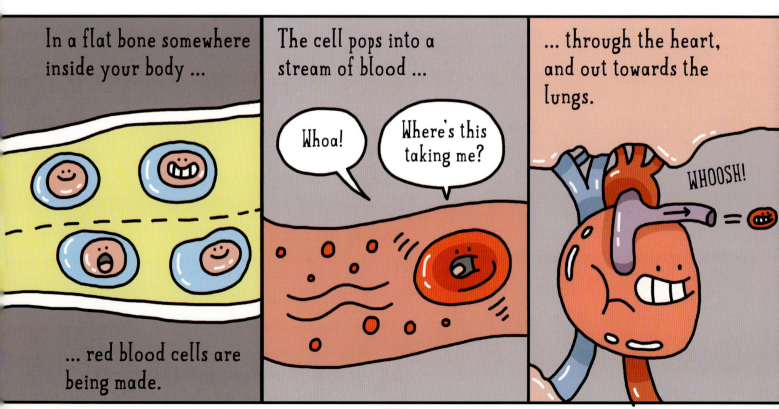

In a flat bone somewhere inside your body ...

... red blood cells are being made.

The cell pops into a stream of blood ...

Whoa!

Where's this taking me?

... through the heart, and out towards the lungs.

WHOOSH!

HAEMOGLOBIN

Red blood cells take their colour from something called haemoglobin, which contains iron. Haemoglobin helps transport oxygen. There is only a tiny bit of iron in each cell – but there are so many red blood cells that your body contains enough iron to make a nail.

Iron nail

Ten-year-old child

Not equally good at being hammered

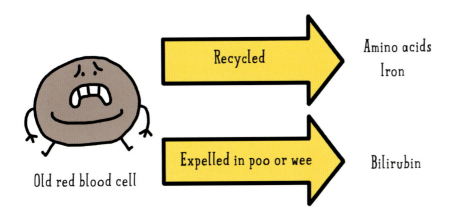

Old red blood cell

Recycled → Amino acids / Iron

Expelled in poo or wee → Bilirubin

RECYCLING

When red blood cells die, they are mostly recycled. They are broken down and most of the bits are sent back to the bones, to make new red blood cells.

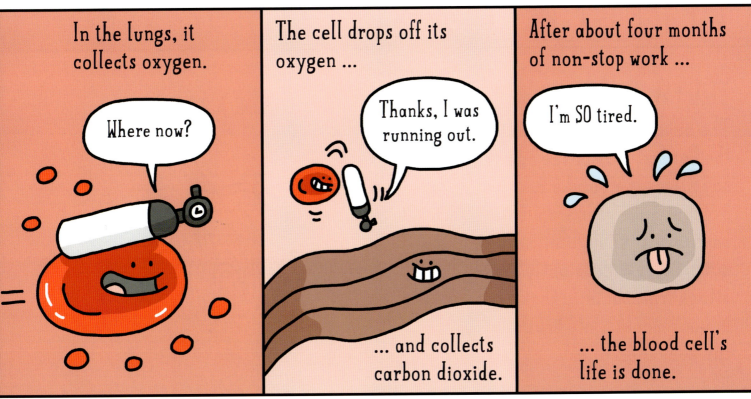

In the lungs, it collects oxygen.

Where now?

The cell drops off its oxygen ...

Thanks, I was running out.

... and collects carbon dioxide.

After about four months of non-stop work ...

I'm SO tired.

... the blood cell's life is done.

THE DREADFUL JOURNEY OF A POTATO CHIP
DIGESTION

Nearly everyone loves chips. But did you ever stop to think about the dreadful journey the chip takes after you put it in your mouth?

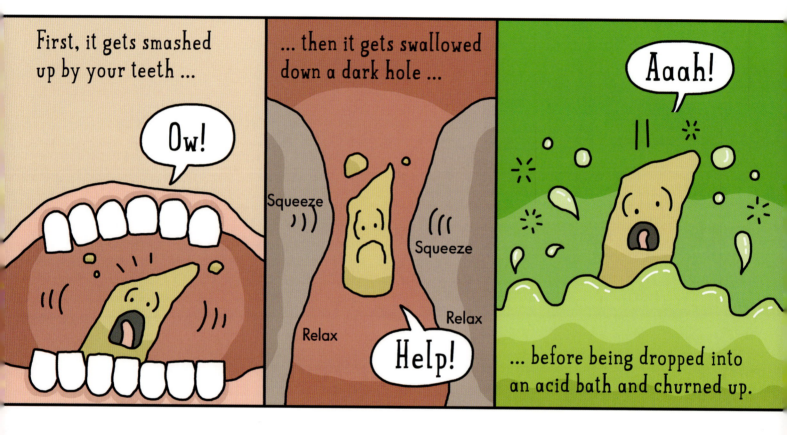

First, it gets smashed up by your teeth ...

Ow!

... then it gets swallowed down a dark hole ...

Squeeze

Relax

Squeeze

Relax

Help!

Aaah!

... before being dropped into an acid bath and churned up.

TEETH

The outside layer of teeth is the hardest part of the human body. This is a good job, because your grown-up teeth have to last you a lifetime. The outer layer is constantly under attack from bacteria that live in your mouth. Only brushing can keep them at bay.

INSIDE A TOOTH

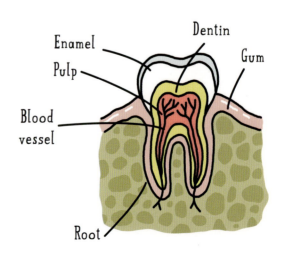

Enamel

Pulp

Blood vessel

Dentin

Gum

Root

CILIA

Cilia are tiny hair-like cells that line human intestines. Their job is to suck the good bits out of food. Not 'good' as in tasty: 'good' as in what your body needs. These good bits are called nutrients.

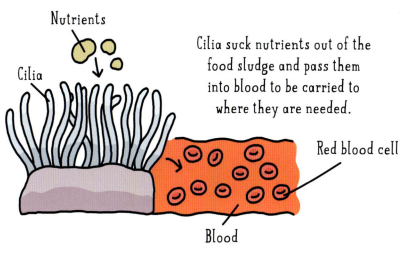

Nutrients

Cilia

Cilia suck nutrients out of the food sludge and pass them into blood to be carried to where they are needed.

Red blood cell

Blood

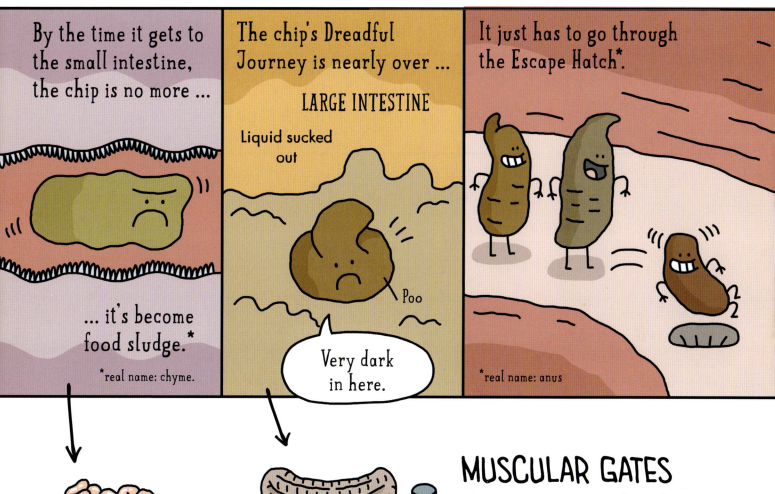

By the time it gets to the small intestine, the chip is no more ...

... it's become food sludge.*

*real name: chyme.

The chip's Dreadful Journey is nearly over ...

LARGE INTESTINE

Liquid sucked out

Poo

Very dark in here.

It just has to go through the Escape Hatch*.

*real name: anus

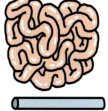

Small intestine: longer but narrower tube

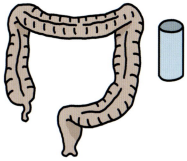

Large intestine: shorter but wider tube

MUSCULAR GATES

Have you ever wondered why poo doesn't just fall out of your bottom? It's because a special kind of muscle keeps the gate shut for you. When poo is ready to come out, your brain sends a message to the muscle: 'Open the gate.'

EATING WELL
DIET AND NUTRITION

Imagine if your body made its own food, like a plant's. You would never have to get up for breakfast again! Humans, though, have to get nourishment from what they eat.

FOOD AS FUEL

Food is fuel for your body. It gives you energy. Just like a car, human bodies need fuel to be able to move. If a car's fuel tank is empty or full of the wrong fuel, the engine won't start or won't work properly. Our bodies are the same.

If you put in the wrong fuel ...

Cooking oil

I read on the Internet that this works.

... it may not work.

Maybe the Internet's not always right ...

SPLUTTER!

COUGH!

FOOD FOR NUTRIENTS

Food gives your body nutrients, as well as energy. Nutrients are the things your body needs to grow, and to stay healthy and strong.

Gardeners sometimes add nutrients to their plants to help them grow.

Use the bag of grey powder.

It is important to use the right nutrients.

La la la.

PLANT FOOD

CEMENT

Oh dear. That is unfortunate.

HEALTHY (AND UNHEALTHY) FOODS

If you want your body to run like a race car, this is what you need to feed it each day:

- at least five different kinds of fresh fruit and vegetables

- brown rice, bread or pasta

- a bit of dairy food (milk, cheese, yogurt)

- small amounts of oils and fats.

VROOOM!

CHUG-A-CHUG FRRRRRRR

But if you want your body to run like a car with the wrong fuel in its tank, feed it:

- plenty of sugary drinks, cakes and biscuits

- white bread (preferably sweet white bread)

- as much deep-fried food as possible.

TIMELINE OF A HUMAN
HUMAN DEVELOPMENT

Humans (like plants and other animals) change throughout their lives. This is a Good Thing: imagine if you had to live the rest of your life as a nine-year-old.

GROWTH BEFORE BIRTH

Humans start life when two cells combine. The cells are a sperm cell from a male and an egg cell from a female. They immediately start growing.

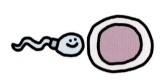

Sperm cell meets egg cell

After 16 weeks: fingers and toes

28 weeks: fast growth of brain

32 weeks: bones fully formed

36 weeks: muscles fully formed

Babies can hear well, but not see clearly.

Waaa!

They cannot walk, or even crawl.

By the time they are two, most children can walk and talk.

I still can't drive, though.

Their brains grow really fast, too.

By the time children are seven, their brains are grown-up-sized ...

If I have to eat a banana I will DIE!

... but they do not think like grown-ups.

Between about 11 and 17, children's bodies take on an adult shape.

Go on. It'll be fine.

Teenagers are more likely to take risks than grown-up people.

By their 20s, humans are physically grown up.

At last ...

PARP! PARP!

Between their 30s and 60s, adult humans slowly start to wear out.

When people get very old the body stops working so well ...

Hearing and sight get worse

Memory and thinking can be slower

Muscle strength lessens

Joint problems become more common

... but ageing does not affect everyone in the same way. And even if they are not as fit and strong as before, older people have lots of useful experience and knowledge.

LONG LIFE

Experts are not sure why some people live longer than others. However, if you want to live a long time, it helps to be:

a) female (the world's 100 longest-living people are all women)

b) Japanese (out of the top 100, over a quarter come from Japan).

GLOSSARY

amino acids important building blocks from which living things are made. In humans, they help build muscle, transport nutrients and prevent illnesses, among other jobs

ancestor relative from a very long time ago

Anglo Saxon people from northern Europe who settled in Britain from about 400 BCE to about 1100 BCE

apex top or highest point

atmosphere the layer of gases surrounding Earth

bacteria tiny, single-cell animal that can only be seen through a microscope

ballistic describing things that are thrown through the air

bilirubin one of the chemicals made when red blood cells break down

camouflaged disguised

carbon dioxide gas that makes up roughly 0.04% of Earth's air

caterpillar larva (the second stage in the life cycle) of a butterfly or moth

cell tiny building blocks of which living things are made

contract pull together or get smaller

clot blockage of hardened blood, for example on a cut or scrape

cytoplasm material inside a cell, which is not the nucleus

dairy food food made originally from milk, for example cheese, butter and yogurt

den cave-like home of a fox, bear or similar animal

digest absorb the goodness from food

drought lack of water that goes on for an unusually long time

energy ability to do work (for example, push on bicycle pedals, light a fire or digest food)

fruit a part of some plants, usually with a seed or seeds in the middle and soft flesh on the outside. Apples, peaches and berries are all fruit

fungus fungi include mushrooms, toadstools, mould and yeast

germination time when a seed starts to grow

gill part of a fish or young amphibian that allows it to breathe underwater

habitat place where living things are specially adapted to live

herbivores animal that eats only plants

high tide highest place reached by the sea as the tide rises and falls each day

impala deer-like animal that lives in Africa

infertile not able to grow crops or other plants

iron chemical that is needed for human bodies to grow, as well as for transporting oxygen in the blood

joint place where two or more bones meet, where the body is able to bend

ligament tough material inside the body, which holds bones and joints together

mate reproduce, or have young

metamorphosis change from one body form to another, such as from a tadpole to a frog

microbe tiny living thing, usually a bacteria, which causes disease

mucus slimy substance that allows objects to slide easily past one another

mucus gland part of the body that releases mucus

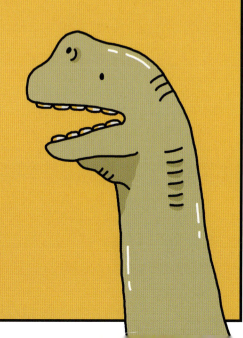

muscle material inside the body which is able to pull together or relax

nectar sweet liquid made by plants to attract insects

nerve special fibre within the body that carries messages

neuron special cell that transmits nerve messages

nucleus central part of a cell

nutrient something a living thing needs to survive and grow

nymph second stage in the life cycle of an 'incomplete metamorphosis' insect

oxygen gas that makes up roughly 20% of Earth's air

peristalsis when a tube of muscle contracts and relaxes to force food through the digestive system

photosynthesis how plants make their own food, using sunlight, carbon dioxide and water

pollen powdery material that is produced by the male part of a flower. When it mixes with the female part of a flower, the plant begins to produce seeds

predator living thing that hunts animals as food

pregnant about to have young

pressure pushing force

prey animal that is hunted by another and eaten as food

pulse heartbeat

regurgitate sick up food

relax soften or release tightness

reproduce have young

rival someone who wants the same thing and is competing to get it

scaffolding structure that supports a building

seed something produced by a plant, from which another plant can grow

species seventh layer of the classification system. Animals from the same species are able to have young together

structure building

tendon tough material within the body that joins muscle to bone

toxin harmful substance

virus tiny object that reproduces and causes diseases in living things (plants and animals)

zero gravity somewhere that the force of gravity is not felt

INDEX

Goodbye!